Brookerytales: Attempt One

Brooke Floyd

BookLeaf Publishing

India | USA | UK

Presentation by *BookLeaf Publishing*

Web: www.bookleafpub.com

E-mail: info@bookleafpub.com

ISBN: 9789358316254

First edition 2023

*To Jesus, To my father, to my mother, to my
sister, and to my sweet Julius.*

I wouldn't be alive if not for each of you.

Thank you for restoring my light.

ACKNOWLEDGEMENT

To my Father,

Thank you for always being completely open and honest with me. I don't know many dad's that would allow their daughter to read, much less use, passages from their person diary.

I love you always.

Thank you to Ashton Taylor with Ashton Taylor Photography for, well everything.

Thank you to Julius, for seeing me through my struggles.

Thank you Mom, for encouraging me to put my words out in the public domain.

PREFACE

Welcome to my most intimate unedited chaotic collective of mental health tales--Attempt one.

Because we all have to start out somewhere.

"She hates Georgia, and perhaps, Me"

My Father's Journal Entry: Summer 2016

"I am so sad! My baby girl just left to go to Colorado. We have argued for the last two months. She was going to leave in July; but she must've tired of my incessant requests to clean her room. At some point, she and I got into a large argument and she was going to leave that night. Tracy has gone with her; I am sick to my stomach. While I could argue about the money I have spent and the bills and mess she has left; I am only left empty inside. My creative, loving child is gone and will be living too far from me. I am so sorry and I feel like I failed her somehow. Her family will grow up without me. She says even if she and Nik break up; she won't move back to the south. My heart is Broken. I pray God takes care of her and Tracy on the journey and in the future. She has no degree and no job. She has sold everything she owns and couldn't stuff into the civic. Could I not foresee the pain I am now in? Couldn't I have just relaxed? Where is my little girl now? Did I make it so miserable? If only we could get along! I love her so much! I am so sad! I planned to ride with them to Colorado. I even looked forward to it. Family is all I ever wanted and I seem to push folks away. I have been working two jobs lately to pay for college and apartment. I want her to succeed. Ultimately, I guess, I am the failure."

"I am 50, nobody understands me; consequently, no one wants to be around me. I didn't help her move-- I just did nothing. I tried to stop her, just until she gets her degree. I am concerned she is leaving because of Nik; and because she wants something different. She says I treat her like she is dumb; but I don't think that. In fact, I think she is smart and not taking advantage of the opportunities she has. I am afraid she is wasting her talents while her boyfriend gets his degree. His mom pays for him while Brooke will have to work hard just to pay her half. She is living with him (something that I wish she wouldn't do). As I said, I am sad! I worry about how sick she gets and her moods. I don't want her to be dependent; I just want her nearby to visit and be involved with her family. Now, I have neither. "

"When I was undergoing treatments for leukemia, she was there. She couldn't do much, but she got me water. She always cared for her mom the most but at that point, she loved me. It

was one of the first times she showed her love
for me. Usually, she would say, "No! Get away!
Mom!" I wished I would have gone with them.
We are supposed to go on vacation to see her in
July. I see Gary's family and his grandkids and
how close they are. I want something similar for
ours. While I am not fond of living in south
Atlanta, I have to stay to take care of mom,
Bobbie. I originally moved here because of the
school system for the girls, although Brooke left
Union Grove and went to another school in the
county. For fathers day she gave me a framed
poem with a picture of she and I,. The poem was
"A Valediction: Forbidden Mourning" by John
Dunne. The we had a "get together" for her
going away! I secretly was so sad that day. I
want to be happy for now, but I am so
concerned. Life is hard and I just want to give
her the education to succeed. Maybe if I was
"easy going" she would want to be near me? I
would give up anything for my family!"

Spring 2017

By the Spring of 2017, I unleashed (un leech-ed) myself from my sleeve. I set forth on a new attempt to find true meaning in this life beyond the mundane. To scream out so loud that the call would then know my name. Perhaps it had bypassed me in my more malicious ways, but that was old me. That was what I was told to be. That was a part I had conditionally agreed to play.

And who was she to condone the accountability of me? I was now exploring out West. Without the church, without my dad. Seeing if I would be bold enough to break away from the atrocities occurring in the south. I was free, but still playing small to fit the scene.

On some Monday in March, Nik went back to Georgia to visit his father. Meanwhile, I cozied up to improbable dreams.

And I danced in discomfort, as I dreamt of alternative mes.
And with no one to make me, I behaved as I pleased.

I sang out the window, from three stories up. Then I sang through Jake's closed door, just to see what was what.

I embraced my frame and erased my name. Poor Jake was very confused.

Either I was somehow supernatural, or mentally deranged.

Perhaps I lived in a broadcast, streaming me, situationally, and all the things I tucked away inside my brain. Or perhaps my dad was somehow involved, monitoring me, keeping me unharmed. Keeping me safe. It seemed I was invincible to circumstance, though it had played its cards many times. There was always some unforeseeable out, a pocket of safety, and I never fell out.

It drove me insane. It felt as if the sun followed me from Georgia just to see my new face. So, I tucked inside to hide. With my gummies to keep me comfy, while I rotted away in my mind.

And it was a combination of songs that finally prompted me to my feet, and I danced until the dance started to take the lead over me.

My Father's Journal Entry: Winter 2017

Approximately a year and a half later, my father returned to writing in his journal.

December 31st, 2017

"Brooke had a nervous breakdown from eating "pot Brownies". She was found naked on the balcony and was checked into a psych ward. Both Tracy and I flew up to Colorado to see about her. She was released two weeks later, but lost her job. Shortly afterwards she moved back home in May. She was diagnosed with Bipolar disorder, and while at first, I wouldn't accept this, I realize it is accurate. After living back with us, she has had several outbursts and mood swings. Commendably, she doesn't want to take medicine. But it is hard on all of us. I try to hold my tongue as I realize she cannot help it. She went back to school for English at Georgia State University. She made (3) A+!!! She studied very hard! I am not sure if she will get on a minor form of medicine in the next year or try to control it herself. As for an English degree, I'm not sure if that will pay her a good salary when she graduates I have voiced my concerns. Right now, I am proud of what she has accomplished given the trials she has endured. She does get sad often because her boyfriend Nik is still in Colorado. He is a good guy and reminds me of Tracy. You know I love my Tracy."

Preparing for Spring 2018

My Father believes in Mind over Matter.

That is the result of surviving over and over and
over and over
You begin to believe in circumstances as
irreverent considerations
Because the matter is made up in the mind, but
when my mind
Isn't quite settling right. I tend to lose sight of
his assertion of mind over matter.

My mind is the matter, Father.

Do you think you could help me with what's
left?

You'll find it somewhere in a pile of clothes,
check my closet.
Towards the back, is where it usually goes.
Pick it up, hold it close.
Find it clothes, and let it know–
I'll return to it soon, that mushy sleeve of bones,
And til then, just help it live, feed it food,
Allow it to rest. Don't be mean, just let it be.

For when I return, it will be imperative that I'm able to clean.

But for now, you take care of matters while I explore my mind, and perhaps I will uncover enough to control all states of mine.

Sleeping Through Summer 2017

What I only now have begun to understand, is that yes there was delusion, with months of unattainable sleep, an intense increase in pressure for me to pick sides in my workplace, a collapsing canopy of alternative narrations I'd adopted as sleeves, and an aching desire to break out of my tower where I suffered greatly, from things nobody could see.

On the days I could, I pretended I was as normal as possible, for dad.

Other days I punished him for holding me to such extreme standards.

Normal doesn't exist.

And for his fixation on making me safe in a world of capitalism instead of safe to break, and heal. But healing requires someone to push you out of the cast, and so I puppeteer through scenarios that best supported my emotional state.

That's how I survived.

How I kept excitement alive.
That is, in my mind.

Upon my return to Georgia, I was so loaded with medical cocktails that I could only find peace during sleep.

 I slept from May 2017-August 2017, when I rejoined the day dwellers whom I imagined to be high on pure excitement for life. I was 23, fresh off rounds of trial mood stabilizers, newly overweight, and absolutely no idea what to do with the never relenting chafing situation that now dictated my daily attire, especially with all the walking and getting lost in the streets of Atlanta. GSU is and was, an absolute maze. And it had come to pass, that I, in fact, no longer recognized my face.

Summer 2011

"Projective tests are assessment techniques that are designed to probe on a deeper level in an attempt to reveal personality characteristics of the child, feelings regarding self and family, and overall emotional functioning."

"An analysis of projective drawings and sentence completions suggest

Brooke
has a lot of interpersonal difficulty,
has trouble understanding her own thoughts,
feeling and actions,
tends to act impulsively
and may be filled with a lot of regret
over past decisions.
She may desire a life that is more emotionally
stable
but have difficulty staying away from conflict,
as she appears to be attracted to drama.
Her life may feel largely out of control
to her."

This was me at almost seventeen. When I first received a diagnosis of ADHD, Bipolar

II-combined type, and Major Depression
Disorder.

My father and my doctor, and eventually my
mom, all decided that I did not have Bipolar.
They decided that the moods could be attributed
to me being a teenage girl. They agreed, I had
ADHD, that was clear. And the depression, well
that made sense. Every woman in my lineage
had carried depression. The family answer:
Zoloft.

Much of the inner personal difficulty (on paper)
stemmed from competing interests of receiving
help and also appearing redeemable and sorry in
the eyes of the court. Whom I was fully
convinced would have access to this report. It
becomes evident in my completing sentences
portion, because I promise you, almost
17-year-old me did not even remotely believe
that being arrested was the worst thing that had
happened, up to that point.

Still Summer 2011

Some examples of sentences on the Sentence Completion Test are:
I am very... "spontaneous,"
I get mad when... "people ignore me,"
I am sort of afraid of... "being alone,"
My father is..."kinda like my best friend,"
I don't know why... "I'm so moody,"
The worst thing that ever happened to me was... "when I got arrested,"
I wish I knew... "how to control my temper,"
I wish my parents... "were more patient with me,"
I wish people wouldn't... "make fun of me,"
I wish I hadn't... "slept with any guys,"
My mother thinks I... "need help,"
I get upset when... "I don't get my way,"
I don't understand why..."I always lie,"
Something that bothers me is..."that I don't have friends,"
Most of all I wish... "people loved me,"
My father thinks I ..."will be okay,"
My mother wants me to... "be a better person,"
My teacher thinks I... "am smart but lazy,"
and In school I... "sleep.'"

I wish I knew… "how to control my temper," I can maintain my face, so long as I'm not emotionally involved with the people in the given circumstance, but let's face it. I am almost always irreconcilably involved, emotionally.

2019

Only through art,

     Written, drawn, smeared,
photographed–was I able to begin seeing myself
     outside intrusions of time, playing elaborate
tricks on the validity of
     perceptions in my mind.

In these captured mes–I could return, remember,
release.

I no longer needed to carry collapsing
considerations.
I could keep them nearby,
Pinned to the wall, or perhaps
In sorted stacks of disarray
Scattered and separate
Impossible to consume
In one sitting.

Never to be consumed without carefully curious
considerations.

An improbable ask, to sift through the riff raff
And refrain from riding the train

In loops round old thrown out tracks,
And to reserve the remnants
Of remembered, or written, parables
From my mind–
I dedicated me to experimentation
For sake of mental health advancements
Of the American Nation.

The more grandeur the scale, the more brave I
become in pursuit.

I said it wasn't for me. It was for the sake of
something far more important, more urgent.

But then, I got a heavy helping of medical
dosing.

The approach? Just shut her up.

But had they listened with curiosity, they could
have helped me piece by piece.

And because no one else would listen to my
detailed derangement of the human arrangement,
I vowed to hear it myself. Trails of tales for me
to eventually tailor and tell.

Once, I find the right mind to assemble clear
lines:

What I was told
Who I would tell
and what only existed in Brookery Tales.

Pre-Psych Ward Brooke

I distinguish in this way, not to be crass, but
because my brain was never quite the same. It
moved slower, lost track, and reacted violently
to the tiniest sensory change.
I lost track of many core memories, and became
so incredibly suggestible–happy to entertain
possible explanations to just about anything.
The more incredulous delusive words I
entertained,
the higher the dosage on whatever meds
they chose to dose me with next.

Trazadone / Latuda / Abilify / Seroquel /
Depakote / Lamictal / Xanax

These are just a peek at some of the medications
that were thrown my way.

March 5th, 2020

My Father's Journal entry

"Yesterday Brooke checked herself into a mental health treatment center. For the past couple of weeks she has been acting strangely. She said she was becoming manic. I guess the pressure of graduating college, having to find a job with insurance and us selling the house must've gotten to her physically and mentally. The night before, she finally cleaned her room so that we could get new carpet. I don't think she has been studying much this year. She seems aloof and distant. At times, she is the sweetest young lady you could find. At other times, she is screaming profanities and smoking pot. We are not sure if she will graduate this spring. Her mental health and her ability to live independently is my biggest concern. Tracy and I are tired. We worry a lot. Her insurance with me runs out in July. So, we are glad she is taking this step now while she has insurance. She seems to always want to have a boyfriend, yet some of the ones she has chosen are not good. Tracy and I prayed that God would watch over her in that place and guide her to find a balance of meds and coping to help her get back to her beautiful, normal self. I miss my little girl. But she is taking the right steps to become a woman. This decision was Brooke's; she came to it after she had some hallucinations, which we think were caused by tramadol. The night prior she was screaming at 4am. Saying she had accidentally killed Brittany's family. Then, she told her mom there was a gas leak and the house was going to explode. She stood outside in the rain. When she talked to the resident doctor at Emory, she insisted that she didn't want medication. But, before we left her she agreed to consider meds if they did not overdose her and turn her into a zombie. My friend Alla's daughter did the same thing. And after a week in Grady she was put on Abilify and is getting better. This all comes among a lot of turmoil. The corona virus is spreading. Stocks are trembling. Crisis seems to be all around. As I have mentioned to Brooke from my favorite poem. "If you can keep your head when all about you are losing theirs and…" in fact, Brooke has the last part of that poem tattooed on her side. Brooke weighs only 115lbs. She is tired and scared and weak. Sometimes, when she is sweet she will hug me and hold on tight and say, "I love you, daddy." My heart just melts for these moments. I don't say it enough, but I love

her "like a rock 'ole baby" and we will always
be here for her–good or bad. "

It's Not A Small Thing

I lose me in the little metal balls clanging
violently, unconstrained. It's
like they're being dropped in a tin—that is my
head—but my head is too small
to fit each panic-filled-ball, compressing some
wrapped-trapped-thing
invading the brinks of my brain. My skin aches
as it begs, for all the boom crashing to
end, those constant vibrations that leave me
unable to think, 'til I break in a rage
against the cage—that is my skull—and try to
rip out the walls from inside.
But the walls are what keep me somewhat alive,
in your
world soiled in desolation, bred in trying to
survive. Sipping not your own
bowled communion of yeah's and I'm fine's,
until all that is left—is an empty bowl.

"It's small thing / to rage inside your own bowl."
—Anne Sexton, For John Who Begs Not To
Inquire Further

The Sun Fell Down

I was standing on the curb of my cul-de-sac
and, it fell.
People ran, but the sun—
was falling and my body was
covered in wax, and the sun saw
ants scattering rampant
with no path. So, I stood
to watch the sun fall,
my bones there to prop me up,
no swarm of bodies,
all tucked in their homes.
Just me and the sun, falling together.
I lay in the grass
and come alive
to the sound of crickets
chirping melodies, of lost tales
Told in native tongue
of how the earth
had eaten
the sun.

March 14th, 2020

My Father's Journal Entry:

Sat Mar 14 '20

"Brooke is out of the Emory Mental Hospital! She has appointments to see a psychiatrist next week and she is taking some psychotic drugs. We are all a little concerned about the drugs and their long-term effect. But, for now, she needs something. She is acting a little paranoid and still has fits of anger. For now, we are not pushing to sell the house in her condition. I don't see a ton of difference, but she doesn't have prolonged episodes of screaming and profanities. The doctors at the hospital wanted her to be a resident for 5-6 weeks. But she chose to be an outpatient after considering our concerns. She is only weeks away from graduating, if she still can. She hasn't contacted her professors since she came home Wednesday. I think that she should do what is necessary to finish her degree. Then, while she still has insurance through me, she can seek more help. Then, she needs a job with benefits!

She owes $40k on her student loans, most of which she spent frivolously on food, partying, pot, etc. I tried to tell her not to do this, but she did anyway! So, her mental condition can be contained while she sets herself up for a future. If she is not allowed to graduate, I am not sure how this goes. She will have to get a job and finish her school, however she can. I love her so much but I am not helping her by just enabling her. Over the past two years I have tried to get her to push forward with school, but she dropped classes and fell deeper into despair. I worry about her!

………..

As I write, Brooke is up and talkative! Which is nice. She says she is on top of her school and "stay out of her business". She is a brat, but it's nice to see her getting back to her normal bratty self. Now, if she will just graduate and get a job! Btw, i am reading what I write out loud to her amusement."

2021

If reality happens to collapse as you are entering a delusional state—the best I can say, embrace moving at a suitable pace. For you, not for what you think you should be able to do. Breathe after each accomplishment or failure and say, how much is too much? Have I eaten today?

Ground yourself as much as possible and let the possibilities pass you by. They're a trap to get you grabbing for things that don't serve you, or your God. Instead try to check in. Not to your brain, but instead to your frame. Don't cast judgment, just observe, look at your body, don't hide from your curves.

Your skin is always changing, and your shape is conditioned by youth. Embrace each new turn and softness you've earned. You've been hard far too long, a softened child, you've survived. You've won.

Eventually your surroundings will come to a similar state: safe, soft, and covered in grace.

And, Again, Summer 2011

"Brooke was asked to draw pictures of a house, tree and a person and answer questions about her drawings. Brooke's drawings were artistic and age appropriate. She drew a house that was thinking, "it is just happy and simple, everything is simple it's a wooden house off in the middle of grass and trees and nature." She said her house needs "hope, its survived throughout the years and still simple and happy." Brooke drew a tree that was thinking about "its just grown, getting old and tired and has a hole for squirrels to live in and its kind of nurturing." She said her tree felt "sad because it seems like everything has been manipulated around it, people put

rocks around it and it didn't want all that," and needs "nutrients." Her person drawing was of a 16-year-old female who was feeling "sad, I think she's lonely, she has a heart necklace on so maybe her heart's broken." She said her person needs "love.""

Cracked Cocktails

I drink the words from your mouth,
Reach down my throat & rip them out—
Cut & paste them to a page
Rearrange the words you claim.

I drench your rants in gulps of bourbon
Slurp them down—like a wad of cotton
clumped in my throat
That I spit it into your hands.

You wipe your palms off on my jeans,
Clean your fingers in my hair
Cut & paste what is left—
To my skin, no longer bare.

I am tired of money.

I want to barter.
Trade offerings of better, and banter
And glamour, us—beneath the clamor.
No cash, no cost, just trading
An act of love.

And I know it sounds soft,
Or, I, sound soft.
Perhaps delusional
Or naïve, for sure lost.

And I am.
In this American plan
To pay penance for gain,
Gathering pennies for pain—
The great American way.

Placating, performing, for public sake
Serving solace, stacked and packed our own
personal place of "fines" and "okays".

Mourning False Starts

False starts in the morning,
And who are you to control me?

The Dawn has come to console me,
Before the daylight must condone me.

And I am stuck in the night time,
Seeking my face without her false "i'm fine"

And if I get the chance to find her
I'll find myself climbing the ladder

Father fare the well
I am sinking,
Almost sunken,
I am barely well.

Father,
I can't seem to eat,
could you help me find
Nutrition I can't seem to think.

Father, I can barely breathe.
The paranoia's come
A creepin'.

And I can't
get to sleep.

Spring 2022

I came home to heal.
I could no longer tend to my physical me.
I was trapped between where I was, and where
my dad thought I should be.

I did what I tend to do, and sought stimulants.
There was too much sorting to do.

I was switched to Adderall, Insurance decided
they no longer wanted to cover Vyvanse so they
forced me to test out another stimulant.

My impulses were beyond my capability to
control.

I tried having my parents hold my bottle, check
my pills, keep me honest.

But, they didn't double check me. And I took it
as permission to continue on doing my thing.

and then I would crash, between wedding I
worked and nights I played with flowers, and my
heart felt like it was going to just stop on a dime.

but no one believed me. They said I was young, healthy. My heart was just fine.

But I wasn't eating, I wasn't sleeping, I was going...going...gone.

My Heart Has Feeling Too.

Longest Tachycardia Episode: OCCURRED during an intense argument with my father. I kept telling him my heart was breaking. It's pure agony to not be seen when you scream the same things, but no one believes.

04/27/2022   5:54:46 pm   #
Beats: 431   Duration: 3 m 1.0 s
Episode AVG: 142 bpm   Range: 135-151 bpm
Patient triggered? NO

By roughly 5:55 pm 3 hours after getting my heart monitor put on, I had my first, and longest Tachycardia episode. I had been audio journaling in my bedroom about the experiment I was running that I was telling to no one. I wanted to see and understand the extent of damage being done to my heart each time I splurged in stimulants just to steal hours back from the day, where I could run about freely and play. Especially not with the flowers I had hidden around my parents house, the one rule my father gave me that I explicitly disregarded. Because flowers made me happy, perhaps I shouldn't have started with ones from the wedding cakes.

An hour into my audio documenting, my dad yells up to see if I was cleaning. And that was it. I lost it. And blamed every self harm tendency on him and never being enough for him. Throwing myself into a tantrum, trying to express what was going on, my suppressed fear was screaming out and pissed no one could hear, and still, I kept going with stimulants and random endearments

43 Minutes Prior--Audio Journal Entry

"Oh, my heart hurts
literally--
I don't know that it's my Heart,
or below.

It's been hurting.
And if I stop, then it just piles onto tomorrow..
and there's only so many more days I can make
it.

It's not as simple as just giving everything away.
it's not as simple as just letting go.
it's sure as fuck not as simple as taking care of
yourself.

no matter how "simple" you make it out to be,
it never will be for me.

I have a hard time recognizing self.

my mouth, my mouth is able to get there quicker
than I
And my mind. It's only after I audibly hear the
truth that I am sure of what it is I have to do.

That's why I try to move at such a fast mode.
So, ill get to the truth before I ruin my life
before I miss a turn.

So I arrive at the truth before it becomes too
little too late.

That I'll still be here.
That I wont miss a single moment of my
peoples' life.
That I am able to bear witness to all the beauty.
so they know that they are not alone.

It has been dark for a long long time, since 2012.
I event stopped being able to recognize the light
in myself. "

Th Audio transcriber couldn't recognize the
words between the intense panicked breaths and
my voice breaking into sobs.

This is what it's been to contain the
"undesirables" of my brain.